The Future Is a Country
I Do Not Live in

"In her enchanting collection of poems, Cynthia Buiza traces "the shape of memories, / the noise they make," with a delicate, uncompromising touch. Her calm, melodious lines push open the doors we tell ourselves we cannot open, doors to rooms that hold what we believe we cannot face — "mother, lover, loss." Distilled from years of longing and griefwork, of solitary walks and communal rituals, Buiza's wisdom is sweet wine for bitter times."
—Boris Dralyuk, poet, translator and Editor-in-Chief of *Los Angeles Review of Books*

"Cynthia Buiza's poetry continues to witness, unceasingly, inviting us to join her in what I call as the last vigil to a passing world, where despite the odds and doubts, she continues to recollect the tracks and thoughts of our fugitive, fragile lives, now enshrined in a foreign tongue she has recoiled and reconciled as her own domicile, a second skin."
—Kristian Sendon Cordero, poet and translator

"What does poetry look like from the notebooks of a life thoughtfully walked? These pages reflect the maturity of consequence, filled by a migrant advocate, world citizen, and a spirit who has held poetry long enough to understand its torrents. Poetry, for those who stroll outside its white walls, is a "miracle at dawn." And there are many miracles in this debut collection – language as a "dance between mercy and grace" – so much thinking, so much survival, so much courage, from a poet who paves her journey by documenting the everyday vanishings and appearances."
—Bino A. Realuyo, author of *The Gods We Worship Live Next Door* and co-founder of The Asian American Writers Workshop

"Many worlds collide in the poetry of Cynthia Buiza, but what remains with the reader are the worlds of the new country vis-a-vis the old homeland. Silt and silk, stone and star, a vast country and an archipelago "with too many names for islands." People suffer and live in her poems; violence and hope commingle here. "She maps this line of desolation from one continent to another…" It is a poetry teeming with images moist and melancholy, "ghosts frozen in the dead eye of memory." The rough-grained world of the everyday and the slippery world of dreams are present, "surfacing in her dreams/ trailed by a lullaby of crickets nesting… in secret places." This is an assured debut for a poet whose wise and wonderful voice deserves to be heard, loud and clear."
—Danton Remoto, author of *Riverrun, A Novel*, Winner of the National Achievement Award for Poetry, Writers' Union of the Philippines

ISBN: 9781734496598

Library of Congress Control Number: 2022935361

Book Design: C. Sophia Ibardaloza

PALOMA PRESS
San Mateo & Morgan Hill, California
Publishing Poetry + Prose since 2016
www.palomapress.org

The Future Is a Country
I Do Not Live in
poems

Cynthia Buiza

Paloma Press
2022

TABLE OF CONTENTS

For my parents, Felisa and Ferdinando

Acknowledgments

No poet writes without inspiration, so I begin this acknowledgment of the people and places that inspired the songs, images and memories that have made it to these pages.

Deep gratitude to Aileen Cassinetto of Paloma Press, poet par excellence, for taking a chance on me, as well as Filipino writers and poets who have paved the way. Some of the poems and essays in this collection have appeared in *Ani*, the official publication of the Cultural Center of the Philippines, *The Philippine Daily Inquirer Sunday Magazine*, *Our Own Voice*, *Tayo Magazine*, *Migozine*, *Chopstick Alley*, the anthology *Filipinotown: Voices From Los Angeles*, and *Verses: A Storm of Poets*, Paloma Press anthology collections and other anthologies in the U.S. I am grateful for their patronage. To my family and friends in and from the Philippines, for your love and encouragement, notably to Rafael Buemia, Allan Schapira, and Danny Tiamzon, who never failed to encourage me. To Victor Velasco, wise co-conspirator, kind, exacting critic and fellow dreamer, friend forever.

To Boris Dralyuk, Bino Realuyo, Danton Remoto, Kristian Sendon Cordero, Luisa Igloria, Eileen Tabios, and Reme Grefalda, as well as fellow writers who believed in me, thank you. To Alan Warhaftig, rock of ages, lifesaver and all-around enabler: thank you for casting big shadows that I may find refuge in them.

Oh, must we dream our dreams
and have them too?

Elizabeth Bishop

We are all on our way
Out don't
Rush

Andrew Zawacki

PROLOGUE

Here it comes again,
the moment when the eye
meets the dare
and sees nothing there.

Is it the tongue of a word?
skin of memory?
flesh of details?
shred of song?

Gnashing at my hesitations
clawing at my womb
where an ancient language
is waiting to be born?

I. REPORTING FROM THE WORLD

SONG OF THE SPIDERWOMAN

It was the faint echo of nothing
or was it nothingness? that startled her.
She looked up, certain the thread
on which she is balanced, shook.

These are her days.
An accumulation of silk but also silt,
All the better to diffuse myths of the mighty weaver.
No one really understands how fragile everything is.

How else to countenance existence woven of slim threads?
What others take for iron resolve takes all of her.
Spinnerets moving in and out of her body,
thin accordion movements that make a life.

Sometimes, she forgets to look up. Like today,
where she just kept going, night, day, light, dark.
Storms, and seismic shifts from the ground below.
It was dusk when she finally emerged from her mighty efforts.

It pleased her that when she surveyed her handiwork,
her cobweb was just as well: thin but tensile,
yielding to the breeze, spanning two trees:
ghostly canopy for the woman who walks below.

AMBER

It is midnight. They have retired to their rooms.

The quiet couple on Suite 723 stayed quiet.
They have long ago given up on the arc of a good conversation.
A pillow the size of a gulf separates them on a bed made of straw.

Zancita on 634 is awake. She stands by the window contemplating fight
     or flight.
She fought all her life. Childhood in a bottle tossed by storms.
Tempests in teacups she drank that never drained.
The choice was easy: flight won.
No one even heard her body hit the ground.

Ana sits by the fireplace inside cabin #6 in the woods.
Her mind is a blank slate. White as an empty sheet of paper
flailing in the dead of winter in the snow.
She goes out and sinks in the cottony comfort of love
below -100 degrees Fahrenheit.

Meanwhile, a creature burrows herself inside tree resin.
She decides that the only way to survive is to stay still. Eyes closed.
Fists clenched against the world. Heart beating.

One day, a subtle wind found her hanging by a cave opening,
glorious burnt siena dazzling even the sun. Incandescent in her shell.
She smiled at the thought of self-preservation.
She was beautiful and impenetrable at last.

AN IDEA OF HAPPINESS

Sun flooding my porch on this whitewashed house
filled with solitude.

It is morning in the place where I was born.
Mesmeric light pouring butter yellow on my lawn wild with anticipation

of a new gardener's hands. Nothing is trivial here. Yet.
Newness rappling through me like the dream

I began building when I was thirteen. House. Garden.
Woman at home in the life she built

after years of losing, loving and losing. It is compelling
that a woman can find what she is really

looking for in a promise made when she was young. I will be "like this,"
she said to herself. Quietly. No witnesses.

Pact made without a fuss. Stored inside phantom
suitcases drifting through continents. Finally arriving.

Even the saddest monarch butterfly
find their way back home, a friend cautioned.

She does not know what time has. In store.
Even the happiest creature understands it is signal

and song that make us dance. The rest she will have
to do herself. And it is just as well.

THE SCENT OF THE PLAGUE

She saw it at 5 am
making its way through the
neighborhood.

Or, did she smell it?
Lush Gardenia and Jasmine
crushed together.

In her village, in the old years
before the pandemic,
the ghost of flowers

haunting her nose
was premonition.
Luck running out,

death announcing itself.
She returned to bed after
bearing witness, soporific.

The sickly sweet smell
of rotting hope
chasing her dreams.

PAGHUHULOS

Moulting: of hair or feathers fall out to make way for new growth

Is the act of tears giving birth to
woman. Liquid pours out of her,
amniotic sac exploding.

A spit of blood, a foam of flowers
the right amount of fear and outrage
and loathing for her sex,

and its cages. Ferrante whispers
in her ears: trust your strangeness
make love to it,

make it pregnant
give it birth. The yes
to the YES.

Walk away from that
gnarly, withered woman
buried in so much mud.

Take your roots with you
to another land made anew
by the fires raging now.

BABY FRUIT

What does it matter that all they want
from her is milk? They will drain her of it
given their appetites.

One thing they do not know are her
riches: forests, trees,
fecund vegetation.

The miracles at dawn
when earth turns to matter
to mineral to stone.

The sun is mighty above her now.
It is making a solemn promise to shield
her from old shadows,

bathe her scalp to sole.
Venus of the raging waters
woman without end. Amen.

HOLY SPECTER

Most of the time, it just sits in a corner,
watching her. She cannot fathom it.
A weight. Dark presence, lump of mystery,
moves when she moves,
and would not leave her be.

Most of the time, it waits. For her. When a throb
of memory thrums in her loins and she grows heavy there.
Warm blood journeying through every inch of skin
liquid, humid, moist as the curve of a neck in the
fervid month of May, on this week of the plague, in Rawis.

On certain days, it is Christ
Crucified, on her back, heavy
as dreams of saints without carriage
cool, judgmental, all wrath and storms,
clanging cymbals and wild barbaric groans.

But today, she tamed it.
Cursed it into submission, saw the thing
for what it was: Chimera. Assemblage of woman and beast
plus, the twenty names for longing immortalized in songs,
in the corner where she prays and feeds her somber afternoons.

DIGRESSION

The woman finally conceded that sometimes
love is like a thousand needles piercing your heart
after it is released from a terrible distance.

Understanding this will keep you from keening
when it reaches the target. Because even a little prior knowledge
will keep the object from irreparable damage.

What does one do anyway? When you feel it coming, place your right
hand on top of your chest, right where the heart beats mightily.
Imagine that you are shielding it.

Imagine that your hand, having held you on countless stormy mornings
such as these, is the hand of a woman certain of her worth and weight in stone,
and as stone, vow to never again be taken for a fragile star.

CORONA TANGO

The first movement should determine the last.
Your finger grazes his face, the perfect axis
for a fierce embrace

of the disease. It could be the dance of death for all she knows.
She made the determination long ago that movement
is the key to staying still.

So she goes on. Looking for love in remote outposts of
this whole, wide, web. Interrupt her funereal days
in languid, cheerless haze.

She stalks the streets, wary of naming
this wanton abandon of spring,
this riot of roses rising, bursting, pretending.

THE CHOICE

She woke at dawn
gilded her skirt with steel
such as the ones worn
by her ancestors.

She prayed before shedding fat tears
the size of olive pits
and bayed at the hollows
of the morning.

What does a warrior do when she
reaches a precipice? Does she talk
herself out of the ledge?
Does she jump?

Or does she fashion a rope
old as the ones she wove many times
in her long march to this place
whispering magic incantations?

Fire, metal, stone. Elements made
for bad journeys and map-less destinations.
No matter. The storm is here.
She'll weather...

WHEN WILL THERE BE GOOD NEWS?

For Rhiannon, who never was

Asked the child of its mother.
She took a deep breath, not knowing
the answer but making it up for her.

When you grow an inch taller, she said.
But how is that so? The child pondered.
How is that good news?

Because Time would have let you, she said.
An inch is the world when it lets you. Be.
One more day to breathe this finer air,

one more hour to watch these Irises
bloom from their hiding. One more time
to enfold you in my arms

and breathe your substance.
She would have liked to tell her
that it's not all about good news

but good things. Enough to eat.
To be in love. To hope for. To believe.
That the day is only as good as the

dance between mercy and grace
mighty efforts we muster between her questions
and the poverty of answers.

EVENTIDE: LOS ANGELES

When the sound of helicopters subside
and the copse of black oak and pine trees
by my window turn from green to dark shadows
moving as lost branches grasping air

my body commences too, the act of slowing down.
Needles stop prickling my skin. The twitch on
my left eye subsides. The nape cools and
shoulder blades rearrange for rest.

Evening in Los Angeles. Home to fervid dreams of home
not here but in another warm location. I look out the
white windows framed by night and track the faint trace
of crickets singing. "Duli-duli" Mama used to mutter.

The sound sits on my right earlobe, lost song
finding rhythm in this, the most dissonant of ages.
It mothers me into memory of landscapes so far
and deep they can only be recalled by replicas of themselves.

It edges me to sleep. Woman sinking deep into reverie
and regret, forgetting and forgiving, leaving and loving.
The many names for islands surfacing in her dreams
trailed by a lullaby of crickets nesting, nesting her heart-

in its secret places.

Duli-duli is the Bicolano name for Cicadas.

CONFESSIONS

"Aim above morality" Ruth Gordon said
in Harold and Maude. Reach for the sky,
those beautiful soft lavender clouds
and crease them, crush them with your palm
or fist or whatever outrage you're into.

Haven't you had enough? Haven't the skies
poured torrents in your direction and drenched
you scalp to soul? Sparing nothing?
Why not rip this fabric clinging to
you like pretense and have at it?

No one will judge. Certainly not this cosmos
and its impersonal jests. Therefore, say yes, to being lost,
to losing it. Some days. To laughing hard at nothing and no one.
Ride that violent freedom called letting go and when you're done,
make funny faces at that woman you just really learned to know.

BAROMETER READINGS AFTER A STORMY WEATHER

There was no guarantee that she was ready for it.
Only that so much bloodletting had already transpired,
and she took a year to sew her skin back on.

She thought transfusions were enough.
But the cycle was unsustainable. Without rain and sea to nourish,
 the woman shrunk so small shame nearly took over.

Heedless of wisdom, she walked the streets naked,
bereft, hair matted Medusa
of the lonely woman of the plague.

She can be forgiven for making up excuses. So much death around her after all,
sharpens the desire to dare mortality. But she knows.
Too well. To keep playing dumb.

She will not wait for anoother weather to break. Right now,
she is parting dark clouds from her eyes; draining tears.
Staring at that ray of light head on.

KURODALAN BLUES

Many years ago, in the heady days of the dictatorship, good things
sometimes happened.
The circus would arrive, Ferris Wheel in its wake, and my village came alive.

The square thrummed with 80's disco. Lights red, white and blue, pulsed
above our dark heads. Visiting stars. Tancho Pomade, its sweet kerosene smell
congealed the air. Mennen baby cologne on her neck filled two breaths.

She was always the watcher. Every time a hand appeared asking her to
dance, she pointed to the anxious girl by her side and commenced her
isolation. Mongrels licked their chops and blinked against a wall of
bodies swaying.

Her solitude in full display, in the middle of May. In a public dance in
Rawis. Sometimes, love and war collided, and a bullet pierced the revelry,
missing its target, killing just the same.

She is caught in this flash of history, at this hour, in the dead of a starless
night in Los Angeles. Alone with her thoughts while the city sleeps, the
faint warnings of an emergency

barely audible from a distance. She maps this line of desolation from one
continent to another, marks each passing minute as though it is her last,
and returns to that night of dancing
ghosts frozen in the dead eye of memory. Brooking no mercy.

**Kurodalan is a Bicolano term for barn dance.*

PRAYER

Lord: where are you? I look around and I see trees.
I try to find you there. Instead, crows find me. They darken the horizon
with their aimless flights. Their cries fugue this city fouled by a disease.

Lord: we need you now. Not later at Holy Mass.
Not tomorrow when the rain stops. Deliver us
from evil men, monsters trying to eat our days.

They say your name yet starve your people of Faith, Hope, Love.
They fatten themselves from the sadness of democracy. They cannot
even begin to understand your will.

So many dead now, Lord. Whoever survives will carve memories of mothers
un-buried, father's un-mourned. Return us to our sense of time. Bless our hearts.
End this world without end and turn this bitter into sweet wine…

REPORTING FROM THE WORLD

It was the mass graves from San Salvador that caught her attention.
Their simplicity: brown earth, rectangular holes, cold bodies, black bags.
She refused for a long time to use PPE in a sentence but there they were,
hovering above the dead, white angels in masks.

Temperature readings from the forehead of children in Decatur, Mississippi
indicated only one thing: many of them will outlive us, ABC's or not. In
beach towns near
Istanbul and Nice, it was business as usual. People swam and swarmed.
The sky was blue. The sea, a shade of teal. Waiting to swallow everyone.

Inside a hospital in Addis Ababa, a perforated lung in an x-ray machine
caught the attention of two doctors.
They could not look away. Long lines everywhere,
 they thought, as they took their time.

Such is the state of reporting these days, she mused. Nothing but news we
already know.
Days rewinding, old cassette recording. Before she went to bed in Los Angeles,
Manila returned to catatonia. She dreamed of mad men in public office
turning all the lights off in her beloved country. She begged the faceless
crowd not to hand them the switch…

KIND OF BLUE

When God made my city, he was in a good mood. He made the hills just the right velvet green to soothe the eye of weary travelers. He created a handsome volcano to watch over it. The volcano had plans of its own.

He made a gulf named Albay, crowned it with cerulean blue clouds so that when humans looked up, what they saw was grandeur on a breathless scale. Paradise found. Blue of the hope of eternal happy endings amidst constant threat of unfinished handiwork.

Except it is all complete. Nature of nature contained within itself. Asks for nothing while demanding awe. When at last he finished with the humans, the tableau was so stark we stood out gnarled, bony stick figures against the spectacular. We went about our business, plucking every fruit we could find. Razing the landscape so we could make ourselves warm. We learned about death, the power it bestows on the living, so we mastered it and killed accordingly.

Made in their maker's image but a complete distortion of intent.

Small wonder therefore, this silence amidst a plague, a flood, monsters in high office. The line of beauty stopped not when a naked, long- haired woman took a bite of the apple, but when choice was born an orphan, and walks the earth with a loaded gun.

BOTH/AND

Is a term of endearment. Twins called love and longing.

She stands by the window, he looks up and her silhouette stuns.
Bent nape lit by this yellow afternoon. Black hair in chignon folds
delicate as a snail curled inside a leaf loved by dew.

"Haja O Que Houver,
come what may. O meu amor
Volte depressa."

She is not here. With him. Always somewhere
else when the sun sets. Sometimes it is a memory of childhood
that takes her away.

Often, it is the absence of the sea. Her familiar.
She moves her arms as though swimming in her reverie.
A gesture to her muse.

She turns around and mercifully gives him the full measure of her attention.
She sees him, whole, full. Loved. But lacking. Like all the holes in her life
long ago marred by bullets.

He has lost her but keeps her. She is safe with him.
Left to her own devices she will drown,
no matter how good she is at swimming.

KEVIN CAN WAIT

He is the shape of my archipelago. Oppressed from the day
he was born. Conquests. Pillage. Revolutions.

An affair with dictatorship that lasted too long. Ancient subjugation
from church and religion warping everything.

He is only a dog in this vast continent of prehistoric beasts. He roams the
neighborhood acting tough. Getting into fights. Coming home bloodied.

Strutting his stuff like the mongrel that he is.
I love him. I don't know what keeps him from completely being destroyed.

Certainly, many have tried. And while it can be said that right now
his fingers grip the edge of a knife, holding on to dear life

he always has it in him to brandish a concealed weapon,
if only to survive another futile bloodletting.

THE SERPENT AND THE INFANT

Was this the image that determined everything? A bright afternoon. All of nine
months old pink to the world, pink toes curling under white cotton blanket.
The green serpent lay coiled on the wall as if riding shotgun. Guarding her?

Waiting? She will never know. She didn't know about dreams then. Just colors
dancing before her retina making her smile, which in turn made
her mother swoon with loving.

This afternoon was different. Who knows how long time held this scene until
it was interrupted? Child and beast asleep to the world. Incapable of harming
each other so long as they stayed silent. When mother entered the scene,

the decision was swift and decisive: get her out of harm's way and slay the animal.
She will never know why she was not harmed. The beast is long dead
though the memory of their brief time together persists.

Her mother tried to spend her entire life
snatching her daughters from predators.
Until she couldn't.

A NIGHT DRENCHED IN TEARS

freezes the horizon.
My mind's eye grazes this icy
firmament.

I consider its dare: walk towards
the cold clearing and you die
of thirst.

Ice will not thaw yet it will drink you
pull you into dark currents flowing
in its undertows.

The choice is freeze to death
or stay very still until the sun
comes up to warm the furnace

of your still beating heart.

MANUAL FOR DROWNING

Enter the water. Drown. Drown. Drown.
Until oxygen shuts down.

Dive. For saltwater pearls.
The rough kind.

Requiring no cultivation. Could live
in this wild woman's marshes.

Swim. For or against the current.
Doesn't matter. Swim above

the corpses beneath. All that loss.
Sing to call your name back.

Float.

I BURY MY LOVE

in the deep of night.
Here where midnight hour
gathers the losing and the lost

who walks among the ruins of the day?
no Eden here, just stark reminders
of desire's devastations.

In the light of day
it finds me wanting,
inadequate.

I burrow my heart deep within sleep.
Here where dreams are cruel
as icebergs cooling and cold.

I roam among sleep's ruins.
Persephone in Hades.
Woman losing and lost.

AUBADE

Is adieu. The last gasp of darkness before light varnishes everything
with the threat of new memories arriving.

It is the song I sing for you, bird of my heart soaring above reason
and horizon so that this dawn is singing too.

The mighty struggle of junctions collapsing,
me in the middle of a bed I made for myself

& condemned to sleep in. Let me wait for the dawn, then.
Let me stay awake lit as a flickering

candle in a room filled with motionless shadows.
This is the room where I wait for you. Borne by an arrow of time that

will never arrive. The hour is past. Sun eager to please.
My eyes flicker at the thought of new memories arriving.

AFTER ELIZABETH HARDWICK

It is July. This is what I have decided to do with my life:

1.	Survive. The harsh light slanting through my window, arrow headed for a bull's eye, me at the center, leaning towards oblivion, alert as a target eager to be spared.

2.	Walk. Stealing the souls of Montana roses in my wake. Grateful for their beauty and indifference. Nothing is ever lost between us. It is just as well.

3.	Move. To a hostile climate. All the better to never ever want anything again. Because certain dreams died long ago in a country oblivious to its ghosts.

4.	Still. The revolver heart of this chaos rising and falling in my chest, tuned to the hours and days I cry: whenwillthisbeover whenwillthisbeover?

5.	Exhale.

THE PEACE OF SMALL THINGS

The song calls out to the woman. An admonition.
She can't tell where it comes from. A white dove the size of
two outstretched palms sweeps down from a height
without warning, disappears into a copse of trees.

The mist has now descended deeper into her mind.
It has covered every aspect of this vegetation
where she yearns to build a life infinitely smaller
than she ever hoped possible.

Meantime, animal sounds prevail over the land she calls her own.
If she could tell you their message, you might count yourself lucky.
Nothing is ever so simple as to merit our lack of enthusiasm
with the familiar. The cool breath of Amihan can stop a mind from racing.

It soothes a creased brow worn from ceaseless grieving;
travel to the heart where it can find the grace she is after.
"Come up for air," the wind calls. Take enough to last you through
vicious storms brewing on the horizon.

When you return, kiss the land that whispered
in this hallowed moment of seeking: "it is going to be alright."
Every gentle and violent creature around contrives to remind:
You are enough.

*Amihan: In the Philippines, Amihan refers to the season dominated by the trade winds,
which are experienced in the country as a cool northeast wind.*

II. THE BLUE OF DISTANCE

If I defer the grief, I will diminish the gift.
Eavan Boland

THE BLUE OF DISTANCE

If you were alive today, Felisa, I would tell you how much I miss the rain
        in Rawis.
Its ferocity the beat of a thousand fingers drumming on the skull of our house.
Then the sudden, cleansing silence.

You would say: "I hate the rain because I never could dry the laundry."
I would laugh at my ignorance. I never understood why you saved old things:
torn clothes, the hint of infinite losses, your daughters' milk teeth stored
        in matchboxes.

Habit not memory, is the problem, we agreed. And in this blue afternoon
8,000 miles away from your grave, I remember. I scatter your ashes once
more in this endless horizon farther than the eye can see. And I assent,
assent to the day.

BELOVED

It is always evening here where I summon my beloved
her hair grown so long, the dark roots of her dark end
falling, fallen on the floor of her grave.

I run my hands through her sleep, her silence silk,
permanent, keen – words I do not quarrel with
because they mean what they mean.

I summon her, telling stories of my faithfulness
how, long after she left, I'd light every candle
set the house on fire, fanned by childhood,

blood, memories, 'til the house quivered,
a star from where she waits.
Fat lights of this fat constellation

pretending they could illuminate a life
darkened by years of yearning.
Longing, ebbing, turning, returning.

SONG FOR FELISA

Because I buried her everywhere
I see her in the still waters of Donsol
moving coolly among schools of fish
pooling at my feet.

She is in the clouds looking at me
in the moment of breaking
in this hour of grieving
one more time.

There are days we dance around each other
like strangers
Daring to remember.
Daring to love.

She admonishes me from
a nether world I cannot know
Yet on days like these
I follow, oh, I follow.

GRIEFWORK

There is a room in my house
that I cannot open
because it contains everything that you are:
mother, lover, loss.

I have walked a hundred times
towards it
I have paced the hours
and felt the keys in my hand like an amulet

but I retreat.
I flee as fast as I can
live again like everyone else: tending the children
loving the husband, writing the poems.

Trying to forgive wholeheartedly
a whole lifetime I cannot face
anymore as I grow your hair,
wear your clothes,

sing your songs, and become your hands
that grieve the gathering dust
in the room where the key
never left.

A PRAYER FOR MOTHER AND CHILD

It has been a long time since we saw each other.
On the phone, your voice crackled
like weather breaking into a storm
and all I could do to keep the tears from falling
was to clutch the receiver mightily.

It was not always like this between mother and child.
There were sunny days skipping rope over tragedies
held at bay by a mother's hand.
Days that lasted like years
making years look like happiness unbound.
How I loved you then.
The sweet of memory of your hair.

Oh, the mermaids in San Antonio have drowned.
Their songs now entombed within your deepening silence.
Witches licked the marrow
of this little girl's tears.

THE CRUELEST SORROW

is imagining you
sad and silent
sleeping as though you willed it
and I, helpless, feeble in my chair.

It is looking at the sun
and seeing us there laughing
like the two desperate women
that we are

and I, dreaming that one day
I will walk into your bedroom
kiss your forehead
and say: Mother, I've come home.

But my mouth is filled with sand.
My tears won't ebb.
I break with the tide.
I recede with it.

It is April.
The cruellest
month
of all.

THE SCAR

it is a black spot that sits on your brain
dark grudge sore from your sorry fall and it will stay

as a reminder of so many things lost
but not missed. Sometimes it hisses,

a snake that rears its head in the dark night as
you flee to another life stepping on dead cockroaches.

The snake doesn't hurt you.
Its shadow makes you bleed.

SELF-PORTRAIT

My mother was smiling when she died.
She was still in her garden as well
and all that was in it
made sense.

She smiled at the sunlight, perhaps knowing
it will never see her smile again.
She pinched a thorn from its stem, perhaps assuming
she will never bleed from it again.

 It was a glorious day, indeed.
The smell of death
made so much sense
she mistook it for good news.

When the day's chores ended,
she folded her hands and sat.
She thought about her life beside the window
and made one last effort to remember it.

HER LANDSCAPE

Because she knows that it always ends like this:
The day, weary of many remembrances
heaves a sigh of moths and walks home quietly.
It passes monumental scenes:
The sun still burning on the pavement
warming the look in her eyes;
children, noisily kicking their heels
humming from school,
and the old women calling after them
to be careful, be careful of things they do not yet know.

It is at this time when the empty road stretches
toward the sky and never ends.
It breathes. It pauses. It hangs
and completes its magnitude
eager to claim another witness. Maybe a hapless
traveler walking away from his dreams or
a keening woman haunted by the things she has seen.

She knows that it embraces all things.
Including the night that chooses no one and loves nothing
and the day that turns and tosses in oblivion
like a ball of sadness waiting endlessly in the dark;
closing and opening consuming nothing but itself.

DEATH ANNIVERSARY

Today, I tried hard to avoid familiar things.

Flowers for example, that remind me of mortality;
the flat iron that used to burn your hands;

the corner of the house where you waited for happiness;
even the family you died loving.

Instead, I distracted myself with strange obsessions
I read a book backwards; I hugged my right foot tenderly;

I crossed the road evading suicide;
but sorrow made me vomit anyway.

THE FLAYING

Grief is staging an uprising
anytime now, it will march through
my brain past my earlobes
and then back again.

It will circle my heart and measure my bones
before aiming for the marrow.
When my knees grow weak it will swim
upstream looking for my soul

and,
failing that,
sit on my spleen
until I scream.

SAD CORNERLIA'S AFTERNOON

The bodies of dead people keep turning up in my backyard.
This morning, one corpse bore the marks of a tortured
childhood turning purple in its severed hands
another, still pink, is still dreaming.

Their arrivals mark the passing of the seasons.
Last summer, they came in yellow and green sadness
and the smell of the sun on their hair
the way their mouths gaped

showed signs of interrupted laughter
one girl who still hugged her teddy bear
was saying goodbye
when she was taken.

It is a sorry affair, this attendance.
When the rains came
their dark raincoats had white holes
in their pockets

hands clasped each other
with mortal strength
making me wonder if they prayed
before they died.

III. TIME WARP

UNTITLED

It looks like an ordinary afternoon, but it is not.
inside my house it is already dark
and I am getting ready
for another invasion:

Sometimes you come to me in waves
of nostalgia waiting to happen.
Sometimes, faceless, I imagine myself
screaming before your bloodied heart.

But it can't be helped.
Cliches' call for absence to make the heart grow fonder,
while I grow tender and shallow tracing your absence from my bed,
feeding this famine with your ghost.

Yes it can't be helped. Time sits with me,
an old river mocking my comfort with solid land
as the hand of this poem clenches
and opens at your command.

TIME WARP

You are always the particular lack of an ordinary day.
Last night, I came home and blew kisses
in your direction before I closed the door.
You were home earlier than me,

peeling oranges and letting me drink from them
before you peeled me inch to anguished inch
and dislocated me again from my place in the world.
But this was before I remembered how far away you are

before I knew that the days laid waste between us
darken like fallen leaves after a violent storm.
They rot in my imagination like garbage.
Not even my wildest dreams can rescue them.

MARCH 21 A.D.

Today
I looked for myself
in the classifieds
and cried when I saw it altered
changed into a woman I cannot know.

All the secrets I betrayed were advertised
without my name
and my number.
'What a tragedy,' I muttered.

but it is too late
because the paper is old,
the ink is faded
and no one reads it but me.

THE LOVER

Because I betray you
let me regret it now,
while the bed is made
and you sleep there, naïve and kind.

let me count the ways, tonight
that I loved you in the past
when we were so new to each other
we shimmered.

Let me break my heart first
because it is easier
by the time your own tears fall
I would have caught its sound

in the palm of my hand.
'I am so sorry, I changed'
is terse, but it will do.
nothing will, anyway.

But let me plan my journey now
the clothes I will wear —
and the angry words
that will split me in half

wounds that will be scars
even as I disappear
into the embrace
of another life.

SOLILOQUY

Rain.
She is a fog that sits on your brain
She is the child that has waited for you since
she was thirteen.
when you never came, she invented a face
and mistook it for love
when you took her hand in dream
she kissed it with blood on her mouth.

She is a fool. She strings her pearls
with thread. She loves without a trace
except she once lay in your arms
and loved you there for a hundred years.

Mi amante querido. where shall we go
without being found?
Where shall we worship without
being condemned?
You are my altar, I am yours.
Without this faceless God sitting in our hearts
this life is useless
like the untrammeled road. Without this burning,
this flesh is shapeless as a spinster's lust.
Oh, I am heady with brutal guilt and shameless tyranny!
Oh, I am lonely like a motherless child!

Mi salvador hermoso. Take me in your arms and slay me
there. Bury me in your mountains and leave me
only with this memory of star and stone.

Rain is a sweet song, but she could drown you,
when the fog lifts will you let her go?

PAS DE DEUX

We are two blades of the same hurt
wandering this edge preparing to die,
whispering our final memories to the wind.

a placeless life. a lifeless love. two gleaming knives
wounding each to each. no comfort here
only an exchange of sighs across the Pacific.

Will you catch my breath when it falls?
will I hold your hand when you let go?
I don't know.

I only know that loneliness will split.
Atom infecting us. A disease. As I cut myself in that
direction, your blood flows in the opposite.

CERTAIN KINDS OF LONELINESS KEEP ME AWAKE

Certain kinds of loneliness keep me awake
while the world sleeps without me
i consume my life without a trace.
i know that the silence that greets me at dusk
is also the silence that i leave in the morning
and it is just as well. i am tired of asking.

i have learned the habits of irony,
the happiness borne of itself.
the quiet downpour of memory,
sometimes smiling like a young girl
who could pierce her life's mysteries,
sometimes weeping like an old woman
who will leave nothing behind.

there are days when i remember so clearly
and i am filled with dread.
because i am running after everything
and everything changes so fast.
like the land of my birth i can barely recognize,
or the beautiful things that take place in Rawis
that i will never see.

but it is just as well.

the 'Banaba' tree in my backyard died a long time ago
but i still tend to it faithfully,
because some things should live for a long time
to help us fill our days.

when the time comes
and i must learn to forget
i will forget wholeheartedly,
including this moment
when loneliness lets go
and silence, silences all memory.

THIS IS HOW YOU LOSE HIM

In cutting out the heart
at night and burying it
in the snow in the morning.

In letting tears burst,
like the rapids hoping
he is drowning too.

In erasures. Photograph after
photograph of imagined cities
you never visited together.

In erasures. Image after image
of fervid nights and tender
mornings you never shared.

In open doors you will walk into
with mirrors that contain only you
so that you can be certain.

In doors you will firmly
close with your hands as you
leave the key behind.

NON-SENSE

While waiting for six o'clock
the ghost train suddenly stops
unloading people and hats
birds and bats.

The women are plump and pale
the men look like Rene Magritte
but their breaths are stale.
What a sale!

This pomp of gray and gloom
this rumpus of life's mucus!
hocus pocus?
hullo! would you care for a cuckoo?

She just burned her nest
first rate arsonist.
I won't tell
keep her there

until my train arrives
on time
dressed like a gentleman
humming a funeral tune

but what the heck
I'm in bloom!
I'm dressed for six o'clock
and I won't take it back!

TRAFFIC

Lately, I find myself easily tearful.
it all began when the peso nose-dived again
and finally broke its nose.

At dusk, the acacia tree in my front yard
shivered, a portent, while a tear in my left eye fell too fast
like something running for its life.

I find myself too, sighing too much, as though my lungs
are all that's left tangible. It is worse when I see the moon
over Mandaluyong at nine o'clock. Jack-o'-lantern,

sinister yet kind, or when I read the graffiti at the tragic LRT
bound for its mission to end all traffic if only we'd stop moving.
Yesterday, I spoke with two Batanguenos who came to Bangkok

to pick apples in Sydney. They never made it past the detention center
and they are homeward bound chewing on grass.
I don't know. My sighs are growing longer than my patience,

I shiver like a tree inhabited by carrion crows,
while my countrymen hang their pockets in the clothesline,
waiting for monsoon to end.

DIGRESSION II

> *To win? To lose?*
> *What for? If the world will forget us anyway.*
> —Czeslaw Milosz, *Return to Krakow in 1880*

To find, Czeslaw
to open your hands and smile
because
looking at them for the first time
they seem to hold you.

To feel
that your body has finally agreed
with itself
because every bone in it works
like a symphony.

To seize a moment
like the right answer
and understand at last,
always,
for the first time.

COMPOSITION 2

You came out of this woodwork
because of deep loving
idol carved by my own hunger artist of nostalgia.
Built piece by piece not from clay
but from memory, stronger than fiction.

You are masterpiece of desire willed to life
by a shift in the weather, a rumor of earthquakes
inside this woman's heart
her own Eden complete
all in a day's work.

A FEW WAYS OF LOOKING AT WEDNESDAY

I.   She is unwell.
     He is weary of happiness decoded
     in small,
     trivial punctuations.

II. Now, he is like rain.
     Over there, a winter cloud is shaping his Thursday afternoon
     making it look like a bad decision
     making it seem like a good day for staying still.

III. Here, a woman writes without purpose,
     biding her time and private cacophony,
     fish flying on water
     dreaming she is fish that could swim.

IV. She is awake, all the time.
     Thinking of you thinking of clouds trapped in marble,
     thinking of white noise on faces
     watched by love.

V.   Here is a man, there, is a woman
     their shadows will merge shortly
     blackbirds
     in repose.

SLOW BURN

> *... I should have loved a thunderbird instead;*
> *at least when spring comes they roar back again.*
> —Sylvia Plath

Smoldering at the end
of smoke damning,
hissing heat.

Retreat to your known world then
where everything is predictable
accountable to a fault.

'Saving lives' when you cannot save yourself
from this: Beautiful liar, trapped in a furnace
that flames and flames.

Line them up, these words, like an execution.
Redemption tossed away in the fireplace like used lace.
This woman burns the way your fingers burn.

PTSD

when I am laid here
stripped bare
what will you see
a woman with horns
a woman with thorns
sticking out of her heart
like magnets?

which night will be appropriate for
loving
and for murdering the past
so it won't murder you?

are you my kill?
shall I plunder you with skill?
will you break my heart in two
and find a woman made of dust
the crust of her convictions
mired in rust ....

you have no answers I presume
so let's resume.

CAFÉ DE LA RÉGENCE

He must not be forty
slender, warm blonde
with a day- old beard
decidedly French.

He knows from doing
this all his life
that every customer
is an audience.

Therefore, a gesture
that takes a page from Delon
is par for the course
and apropos.

In a place where flipping
plates and flipping
styles are an art form
as I just recently found out.

He holds my gaze
I linger in his,
lingering like the mad woman
that I am.

Always suspended
in my imaginarium
desperate to pierce the mysteries
of my own thoughts.

After a moment's
pause I gave in, I waved at him
and very un-French like
told him he forgot to salt the cod.

MY QUARREL WITH YOU

'So we are grasped by what we cannot grasp.'
—Rilke

I have a fear of descent.
This afternoon, at the London Review of
Books Bookshop, I saw myself tumbling down a flight
of stairs while I clutched the banister to
use the loo.

As I fell, my neck broke and what landed
at the bottom was a heap of clothes.
I watched myself crumple
dirty laundry at the foot of my life,
clutching Olga Tocarczuk's book on flights.

This always happens.
No banisters powerful enough
to stanch the stench, metallic in my mouth
blood pooling just under the papillae.
A taste for death.

A woman, one way or another
is always falling.
Damned damsel in distress
falling down some stairs
or out of love.

I do not heed the warnings of vertigo
so I skim edges to test
the limits of martyrdom.
And failing that
pretend that stairs are for climbing.

FREEDOM

I just want for a moment to live without your disapproving
gaze. To wade in that water, too salty, too tropically warm,
and decide whether drowning and waving are two sides of a coin.

You see everything has a catch. Love blooms,
romance fades. A good marriage lengthens into oblivion
and you are two astronauts lost in space.

Even death cannot be cheated for too long.
Those gravity defying acts you performed
 always had an expiration date. Time stamped on it.

Where does that leave us? You asked.
I stand up, open the door, breathe the air.
Already I am thinking of the blue of my childhood dreams,

of swimming as flight on water. Already my feet are wet.
A ball chain the size of your wounded heart grips my ankle.
As to nowhere, I go.

JUST BECAUSE

It is deep summer here
and I don't know the weather you're having,
even though I know it always rains where you are in August.

I am counting the days when I say, with a gesture I haven't given, lately
        to anyone:
I have waited for this. To look into the deep pools of your eyes
and not see a photograph but see the man.

Just because I wait doesn't mean the days are not heavy with your absence.
I want to pierce the mysteries of longing, carve them in my loins
and walk with the pride of a woman freed from the limits of captivity.

It is deep summer here where your name is etched in the Birch trees
I pass by in my endless walks around this city. They whisper your name to
        the wind.
Three beats that make a breath. And breathing, survive another day.

IV. EVIDENCE OF EXILE

Your absence has gone through me like a thread
through a needle.
Everything I do is stitched with its color.

W. S. Merwin

Perhaps life is a long avenue a woman with a basket
crosses everyday.

Forugh Farrokhzad

THE BRINK

Sleepless,
I put on my boots and head for the sea.
I walk with the purpose of a madwoman
out to argue with mermaids.

I pass my childhood by and make faces at it
careful not to interrupt its psychotherapy.
I wave goodbye to my mother and tell her that it is alright,
everything has been a wonderful dream so far.

She begs me not to walk too fast
nor drown too deep.
But it is late.
Very, very late.

EXILED PARTS

My tongue has left my body
it has moved to Spain to dance the flamenco
and flirt with madmen.

I was asleep when it packed its bags
and stole my jet-red shoes
sticking its tongue out, making me dream of lost syllables

unraveled pearls falling from my neck.
Its absence hurled me to a country colonized
by a dead language mutating in several continents.

I miss it. I miss its obstinate flicks
how it gnarled at my inadequacies to remember
the songs of my ancestors.

This tongue that lost its head.
The head that lost its mother.
The mother that lost its land.

HOME ALONE

The mornings are hardest
when he leaves and she inherits a house
draped in silences
and a backyard dappled in California light.

The hours climb her body like a horror
a certain tremor in her limbs, a stampede of ants
threatens what she has come to know
as her footing in the world.

She reels the tremors in and surveys the basics:
a broom poised by the kitchen cabinet
dishes stacked and cracked
the furniture rigid, menacing.

She assigns a certain resolve
to the act of keeping house, a partitioning
of her will, the wailing wall of compromise
rituals of patience growing tedious by the day,

as she wakes to the same California morning
over and over again,
and disposes the husk of a missing woman
into storage.

WAITING FOR THE POEM

It is late again
I know because I am counting my breath
I am still twelve years old
and the rain from my window is bigger than my thumb.

There is so much to forgive but life keeps missing
like the train to Legazpi that never leaves.
Oh, Felisa, what time is it?
Can't you see the clock on the street?

It does not wait for me.
It keeps moving within its absence
like the devil lurking where it lurks
in poems that do not arrive.

CROSSING THE ROAD

—for my sisters back home

if three of us cannot cross this road
and one will fail
what will prevail?

your hand rocks four cradles
while he bays by fortune's rocks!

you spin cobwebs on your hair
and wait for tarantula's to breed?
fuck this town you said
but you don't want to leave
wedded to bad nostalgia
captive to toxic metaphors.
your beloved city is the ghost
of a bastard called legaspi.
the voice of a dead oppressor
still calls you Indio in his grave.

so let us then forgive each other for standing on the street.
for missing the signs, for shuffling our feet.
you might go east, i might head west.

i love you, we are all in this together.
but a speeding truck might put asunder.

OUT OF PLACE

Where I live, it is not even winter
but something else
vacant, a shade more ghostly than
a pale hand exposed.

Where I am, it is getting dark
with the patient accumulation of
blood in bathtubs
and deaths delayed.

Yesterday I tried to leave.
I sat on a bench and planned my exit.
Routes I hadn't taken before
hoping to arrive where I am always wrong,

but certainly proved.
Still and steady as a corpse,
looking out the window towards a world
that does not look back.

EVIDENCE OF EXILE

as a woman to her mother
will promise
as a child will reveal
the house is no longer there
but it houses her still,
place loved by this woman's body
no longer that child,
but dreamer of lost things in lost countries
flickering north of her quickening memory
no longer here but in another life
gathering storms and stars that are not stars
but years, accumulating in this little girl's face
when mothers were young and their songs were songs
not voices that keep sleepless women
from sleep.

THE ARC OF NOSTALGIA

What do you see here?
Said the child to her father
pointing to her small hand.
He said: 'you would leave, that's what you would do.'

She formed a circle with her index finger and her thumb.
His eyes glistened like a man who fought to understand.
That was thirty years ago, the girl has moved on to her questions
Past an old man who did not learn to forget.

the inevitable.

LEAVING

I am tired.
Birds have built a nest in my hair.
Spiders
are spinning lies in my heart.

There is no time to start
again.
Time is the sun
receding from my window.

Sun is light
trapped in stone
ochre, opaque
monochrome.

There is a drone
in my head
which refuses to
make its bed.

The ghost
of my life
prepares to die
instead.

CYCLOS

Last summer saw us feeding
our small lives
with small lies
'til we grew fat as snowmen
and as lonely.

Winter was something else
kept us indoors
waiting like a tumor
purple and malignant.

When spring finally came
we asked autumn to carry us away
saffron leaves
into oblivion.

AFTERLUDE

and then the flicker of the lamps
quivers on the street
and the night begins
its slow descent to etiolate

fading into her
creature alone in the gutters
of her grief
staring at a rotting peach
peddled by a mute senora on the street.

'flores para los muertos!'

her ghosts are singing each to each:
come now little girl blue
the time is now
for you to come along
the streets are ready
the night is only in your eyes.

but they are wrong
every single spatter
every noise and clatter
keeps her in this room
no one claims her but herself
and the shifting of the lights
when dawn carves her face
into solid shapes of gloom
and she folds the night into oblivion
with the lights, and the room
and the scattering of the moon.

morning returned to itself
with all its blinding sense
and confidence
erasing her like a lie
tomorrow is another pyre
in which to consume herself.

DUSK

There it is
the house is veiled again:
silence.

On a distant island
drifting farther away from her
a murmur of desire

make the trees shiver.
A sadness, a weight.
The world

its habits of forgetting
give trees, their shadows,
their unbearable gravity.

Cara-caran,
the name is a familiar
it never left, it goes where she goes

refusing to forget, demanding root as mortar.
And moor. Without it, the woman is
a ghost at best,

searching for the nine-lettered word for home
scavenging the world for her place in it.
World waiting to be born.

HOW TO DISAPPEAR

You are, right this minute
contemplating how you would disappear
without a fuss,
maybe even leave the TV on, not for effect
but for clues:
What you were watching perhaps,
when you vanished.

Already, I speak of you in the past tense
words always make it easy
when the rest slithers away
incomprehensibly,
such as the time when you were so happy but so poor
or the day when you thought you will never grow old
and easily injured.

But you did.
Forty nine and shaky with infirmities
here a bone aches, there the heart breaks.
Funny how remembering is a pain
always worth the flogging
such as the time you lay under the trees
yearning to melt into their roots
young but already too mortal for your own good.

You hoped to dissolve into the earth like the endlessly
falling leaves, falling and flailing as you went.
Instead you walked towards the sea
walking and sinking until
depth claimed you
and nobody had to know.

AUTUMNAL

Autumn in Legazpi is a bad joke
leaving a cold face.
In a place where there is only rain,

Bougainvilleas riot on broken fences
like a misgiving, too sad for its own good,
too crimson for mourning.

No one can match its instinct for survival
not the woman who paces inside her days like a prisoner
nor the child who looks away from her father in anger.

There are no reasons
for its omnipresence than this:
to witness the steady putrefaction of our days.

PLAYING GODDESS

She had no other choice.
He left, slowly first, then, like a caged beast
who could not wait for the door to open
fled through the cracks and disappeared.

Then light left her eyes for good.
For a long time she closed her doors,
Sealed her windows shut
as wild grass grew around her.

The children crawled and cooed without her benefit.
Daylight slithered and slowed
on dark corners of rooms
without interruption.

She wondered about women in other continents
whose hands were enough to contain happiness
who never worried about unpaid dues
and had their fingers painted red with white haloes.

Hollowed are her days now.
Red is the only color that she mourns
as dusk offered neither
courage nor consolation,

only the thought that one day
she will light a candle to it all
stick her tongue out at false hopes
and resolve to take her life in her own hands.

WALKING IN LOS ANGELES

I keep coming back to a place I have lost
a long time ago when I was already old
and no one in the village knew my name.

The church where Felisa spent
her Sunday afternoons
still asserts its presence:

Spire, dome, gloom.
The pealing bells as the villagers stopped in their tracks
to pick their pockets for miracles.

I've always wished that things were different
possesing too much credulity, ship of fools
even as I know that things weren't always the same.

A neighbor could obtain mercy without a price.
A girl could dream by the window and watch time hang
as *Love In The Afternoon* crackled on the radio.

It was a time when women danced on the square
like it was the only business of living
and young men fished solemnly on Rawis beach

to catch their shadows on water.
All this is lost now. I do not even know who I am when I dream
only that everything comes to me in sleep, and waking, I lose them all over again.

The village of Rawis is where the poet grew up and spent most of her childhood.

AN ANSWER

You say that I repeat myself.
When I talk about the shape of memories
the noise they make,

their procession at dawn
when I dream alone, and waking
find myself abandoned.

What is life but repetitions?
What are words but mothers
that cannot keep us from weeping?

I am tired. If I could carve this tongue
out of my grief
If I could wring my heart out of this hurting

If I could forget.
You will not hear me talk about islands
and twenty names for tears.

Instead, you will hear a noise
quieter than before, leaving you slowly
feather flailing away

an object you lose as you reach for it
because what we cannot keep we bury
and what we cannot bury, we mourn.

FOR C.P. CAVAFY

If while looking outside the window
you see things that are not there
but from somewhere else
look away.

It is a trap.
The leash that takes you
from the yes,
the things you have now become.

But if you cannot look away
if you cannot close your eyes
if your mind refuses to obey your will

you have a decision to make.
You have to accept
that the faces that look at you are real.
That they are not tricks or phantoms

or certain cities you have lost.
Better yet, they are the nectar of your dreams
the ones that wake you up for a reason.
When reason is what you no longer possess.

THE OTHER SIDE

Morning, and what goes on in the neighborhood
is the whole world going on about itself.
bright rooftops, their anaesthetic sameness
their windows shut against mine
saddens me.

I look out the window every day
hoping to be surprised, asking to be forgiven.
I would like to enter these houses
pry their secrets open, tell them about myself
why I am always watching.

I believe that whoever is looking out agrees
that I am not what I seem,
that there is so much more to me
than the eyes that seek
this landscape for consolation.

I believe that whoever knows
the story of a woman
opening windows to herself
so she could shut them down
has seen what I have seen.

JUDITH

It was called Flores De Mayo
and everytime they asked her to play the part
of the queen who would not be just
she obliged.

The woman in red walked, waved
severed head of a severed man on a big brass plate
silken dress that rustled with every stride.
She walked along half-forgotten streets
in Rawis, ravaged by storms and seas that
licked its shores clean of miracles.

She remembers carrying the dead
on that brass plate
like her last supper
feast for a fool
the red dress flaming and flaming
against the candelabra.

As her face gleamed against the glare
her curse, incandescent refused to be proved
so that as the years passed
and the dress frayed
Judith dreamed endlessly of things that would not let go
haunted her in sleep, an animal that refused to sacrifice its waking life
so that the dead could rest in peace.

AFTERMATH

To my sisters, after a typhoon

I.

Before you know it, poems will be written
eulogies said from the pit of grief
not the poetry nor eulogy that you know
but the ones that cannot be uttered.

I am like a madwoman digging
with the rest of the bereaved with my bare hands,
I look for signs that will tell me
all this is a bad joke from a cold, cold heart
except nothing is funny
not that man burying his children with other strangers
nor that widow who threw herself into the rocks
so that everything could be forgot.
What I thought was a smile of letting go
was just the aspect of a broken face
misshapen by tears.

Grief is a weapon against ignorance.
Since I can only watch and follow
I learn my city anew
the disappeared and disappearing
landmarks that will cease to be map
to memory.

My sister's voice crackles on the phone.
She thinks this is the wrath of
a constantly angry god.
I let her speak. I let her anger roar
and roll like the storm that turned her city
into silt.

Who am I to say otherwise?
Who am I to say anything?

II.

They are now among the beloved.
walking away from their graves which do them no justice
they hover above the landscape, their smell still palpable among the
fallen trees. The only sign that death triumphed is the immense silence

that now hangs when night falls and no one looks forward to anything.

III.

Something about the end of a storm changes the quality of light
Renders everything sharp and brutal.
On a clearing today, the dead are buried in one nameless grave.
Their spirit stands aloof, witnessing, curious about the blurry figures
they have become.

Soon, they will be lonely. They will pace the city and prowl its nights
disappearing into corners while people believe they saw someone familiar
waving, screaming, as though wanting to be found.

IV.

Is it possible to ration your sorrow?

I regret the days I let the wind carry your voice away instead
of reaching me. Times when memory is all we can talk about
and I steer the conversation towards the future.

How ignorant of me! Believing that the past is only good as it is useful.
Unaware that it has a life of its own, since it reads your life
without permission
and leaves you wondering why you are utterly lost
once more.

V. LOST WORLD

> *... come celebrate*
> *with me that everyday,*
> *something has tried to kill me*
> *and has failed.*
> *Lucille Clifton*

BIRTHDAY SONG

One morning you wake up and finally you notice:
the few gray streaks by your right temple
growing long, or, better yet, growing old
the art of moving from one face to another
each variation a blunt force self-inflicted trauma.

Every day is a day that the Lord has made
but I do not always rejoice in it
some mornings, not this one, I would gladly hurl my self
in front of a bus or hurt someone with a raging blow
but they *don't know*, so I won't do it.

The point of the matter being
as I grow colder, sadder
as my bones begin to wander
 from my limbs
I am grateful and wistful

I no longer howl at the moon
and count my grievances
I look around me and think: this is it
'This is the day that the Lord has made
I will rejoice and be alive in it.'

WIND AND ASH

My longing for my country
Is like a broken heart.
I am the pour
It is the vessel.

Time travel is the only way
I know to reach her
Memory upon memory
Swimming across the Pacific

Currents of wind and ash
Surviving the waves
Determined to locate
One destination.

I can tell you that on merciless
Days like these in Los Angeles
I would give anything
To track her shores

Finger her sands, granule to granule
So that I, woman of two hearts
Dreaming in two continents
Can find some moveable peace

In this dislocation.

MONTREAL

And if I did not travel with you
know that I travelled too.
Just last night I slayed dragons
in my sleep once more.

I cried. I slashed and smashed.
Screaming 'bloody murder.'
But morning kept only
the exhaustion of so much effort.

In a river that flowed in my dreams
an eight year old tried to drown her self
while I begged her to please wait
it was too soon.

Her village is filled with lonely children
looking for love. So while I am trapped in this mighty will to roam,
my heart expands toward the roads I never travel
and these irises suddenly bloomed in my living room.

ON 1534 FRONT STREET, JAMMING LIKE FRANK O'HARA

Every moment is an act of playing God. Even the computer asks you this: Do you want to save?... Do you want to save yourself today? Brine your despair in brine until it is no longer edible. It might help. The other day, I thought I was soooo good. I made sure everyone agreed (or at least I hoped so) that I was what they have always wanted: glib, slick, hip to the bone. I am pathetic when I am trying so hard to survive or even just merely "fit in." But I kid myself. I go home fingering heavy smooth stones in my pocket and wondering why I haven't tied them into a string around my neck, or better yet, just jump with them in the river. Except I hate drama. One Virginia Woolf is enough for a generation of suicides to make life seem worth living. I need. To. Save. Myself. From pity. It is tough when a quarter of the memories that dwell in your brain are damaged, they refract within cracked mirrors and you don't know whether pity is your enemy or your friendly neighbor. It's fucked up really. You travel for a long time, thinking that your journey has been amazing except there is that one clearing where it seems like an alien spaceship has decided to permanently spot a light on. So you stand there, frozen in 21st century real time, looking at the woman who looks like you stare back at you asking to be saved and no god nor computer to hand you no stones.

THINGS WE LOST IN THE STORM

If you have ever wondered what you have lost when the wind blows like
the *amihan* with no mercy, you will know if you lived here. A murmur
smoothes your nape like a bad longing. A commotion in the ricefields. A
disordering of leaves. The lizard ticking on the roof of your brain.

One morning I woke up and I finally found what I have been missing: I
have no photographs. There are no more tigers that roam in my sleep.
Once, I strung them together in a jungle of verse and wept when I cannot
find the words because they are gone, all the smiling faces.

Everyday is an aftermath of the storm. There is nothing to it. Whenever I
force myself to look, that is all I see. Scattered pieces of news, the
Gumamelas in her sundress, his sad hands, the chair's misshapen legs,
dolls with no heads, islands and houses in darkness that is only from Bicol.

Felisa, Simona, Pedro, Ferdinando…
Woman with no landscape, only mirrors.
It is a terrible fate to lose landscape in which to roam. To lose my bearings
in a continent that won't bear me out. To smile, ruefully, at regrets. To itch
of too much loneliness.

The storm is a lonely hunter. It gathers me in its arms and flings me over
cliffs and rocks and waves and tide pools whose terrains — I plead, I
bleed. It is already midnight.

WALKING ALONE

Anything can happen with a woman walking alone.
In this golden, glinting afternoon
In this wily, willing street of stores made up for Halloween
she wondered if it is possible to finally meet the answer.

Once she thought the love she had always wanted
the one she hoped for, prayed for and obeyed
in the corner of the room where she hung a garland
of jasmine blooms, waiting

for signs that made her believe
could save her and sweep her away
from here.

Nothing happened. The days obliged with their hallmarks
of surprise and disappointment. Deaths, births, cousins, friends,
pool parties, hot air balloons
the arts fair that took place every winter.

On the way back, she could not ignore the approaching truth rising towards
her from the pavement, on this bright and cheery Florida afternoon
as pedestrians eyed her coolly.
Grief claimed the maiden too soon.

NOCTURNES

On a night that keeps the neighborhood awake
a tremor tears through the walls
a sigh from someone alone in his bed
stirs a leaf.

No. 8 is rearranging furniture,
careful about the sleeping dog lying on its paws
and the neighbor to the left
snoring through the roof over our heads.

No. 6 is dreaming
her legs paddling
in quick successions
fleeing a mighty shark.

Outside, the moon watches
behind the clouds
its stillness send the trees 'a quiver'
it is so tired of being awake.

Meanwhile, the poet slaves away
firing words like cannons
aimed at the approaching dawn
and a useless gesture called a yawn.

VEGETAL

You smell it.
The body's fall season.
Not the hint of oakmoss in the air
but the moist rot piled under freshly fallen leaves.

This season, unlike winterspringsummerfall
doesn't end because it is the beginning of the end.
The way suddenly your knees and legs are no longer
the racehorses they once seemed to be when you were twenty-three.

Or how your eyesight keep reminding you
it's turned 50/50. But it is the smell
that warns. It says you are from earth
and this is how it claims you:

> *Without ceremony, it wafts, lingers, where the limbs begin.*
> *Vinegar, chemical, corporeal.*
> *Scent that is not of this world but leaves of your flesh*
> *commencing their etiolation.*

Your world ends not with a bang but with degradation.

HAI KU (OR HAY NAKU)

The city from 2,000 feet
is the ruins of a civilization
rather than the flowering of one.

I cross Kalayaan Avenue
into Burgos. His beggared five- year
old hand beckons.
I am home.

BLUE THURSDAY

She likes blue. Any kind of blue.
But this.
It is only 9 o'clock in the morning but the day
has already ended.

She is inside a blue bowl called Southern California sky.
Cerulean. Obsidian. Indigo.
Midnight blue raving
the size of a fist throwing punches in her direction.

Even the oak trees outside her window are tainted.
Blue eyed bluebells sing to them from below
sky blue leaves dancing with the Santa Ana's
devil may care.

She'll swim into this day somehow.
Come up for air soon. Blue Jays sing her sorrow to the wind
and she'll sing with them.
Because the only way out of blue, is through blue.

COURAGE

Sometimes when I cross the bridge I see her
just above my field of vision
or under the shimmering cool surface of the water
waiting, it seems.

For every splinter that makes me bleed
there is a memory of her and him
of loves that died
those I murdered, those that murdered me.

Hang or drown?
Grieve or forgive?
Live or
go on living?

What did I lose that is lost forever
that I am condemned to search for it?
At the end of the bridge is a precipice
always asking me to step over but I digress,

I walk back towards where I came from
towards everything
that I already know
the only weapon I already have.

FROM "QUESTIONS OF TRAVEL"

We who are denied nature
anything green and opulent
that turns us crimson with sentiment
what of us?

We who are denied
Ms. Bishop's Brazil her
"mountaintops that spill over in soft slow motion."
what of us?

There is a brook
in my ceiling
a beautiful, white horse
is drinking from it

But it is also a hundred year old pipe
that runs through the city
and can't be bothered
to impress.

Steel cold concrete
makes me want to believe in
terrains and a future
with me in it.

Clouds that travel and tarry
but always return.

DUSKLANDS

She wore the look of someone who and where death has happened: alive
but distant to the present always at the same time. That noticeable
inwardness, coyly hidden but visible just the same; a certain hunchedness
of the shoulders, a resignation in the shoulder blades.

There and not there. Alive and dying.

There is a harbor from a not so distant memory where the dead
congregate sometimes stranded, sometimes seeming to make a home of it.
She visits it every so often, trying to understand why, for a certain period
in the river of time, three members of her family died in one year: Felisa,
Cecilio, Roque; Mother. Uncles.

They are of course nowhere to be found when she is passing through their
territory, choosing to visit her in dreams, when sleep is the only refuge she
could find.

It really was a massacre of sorts.

LITTLE GIRL BLUE

I keep feeling sad for that girl
daughter of ghosts
bearer of mysteries and histories
heavy on her back as wings.

I keep telling her to stop dreaming
take up life in all it's blinding light
and tender mercies.
Fly towards it.

But she won't be consoled.
She hews close to the earth digging
for love, loss, latitudes.
She won't be told.

PUERTO CLARIDAD

You are exactly where you have to be
at rest in the knowledge of this:
there are no more places to hide, this is
the last refuge at the end of your world.

Every question that repeats itself
in the widening circles of your searching,
is merely a deeper
place for you to be found.

Despair no more for desires that
break you at dawn;
cold marble in the bright
light of your morning.

Nothing is new
but persistence and insistence
the courage to live everyday
as though it is always your first.

STILLS

—After Sarah Charlesworth's "Doubleworld"

I don't know what is wrong with me today:
Images of people falling from buildings
make me want to weep.
Patricia Cawlings, did she jump
to her death
or was she fleeing for safety?

The Columbia Gorge is burning
because someone flicked
an incendiary material towards it.
A hurricane claimed an entire country.

It could be that I am, in this helplessness,
merely the unrelenting witness unable
to do anything but watch in horror.
As horror after horror comes in waves:
a madman living in the White House
eating tweets for breakfast.

A country dissecting from within
unable to stop an oncoming train
filled with corpses that have fallen
from tall buildings.

SATURDAY

I don't know whether to write a poem
or clean the house, so much is vying for
my divided attention;
it is always like this.

A minute ago I felt a scar just above
my eyebrow and remembered.
I thought about scars
how resilient they are.

They close their eyes
against my daily tribulations,
dead tissue above my skin
membrane intact.

It was in the midst of this indecision
that I thought of you, and wrote these words.
Then everything, at least
for the time being, is clear.

LOST WORLD

*"She is the girl waiting at the crossroads about the dead hour of the night.
She is your lost bride and the heart's failsafe."*
—David Harsent

His movements, against those constantly shifting arcs are so willful, it made
her wonder what circle he is trying to complete. The way it started is so far
back in time she has trouble looking for it in the distance. Of their past.

She was a girl then. Not much substance to her. Exquisitely lonely, infinitely
solitary. Still. She remembers the long walks to get home. Agoho Trees on
the road to Rawis whose shadows lengthened as the sun sank over the
horizon. Years of walking those roads and not a footprint behind. Today.

She will always believe he saved her. Maybe that was the source of the
mystery that won't be resolved: the act of something in the universe and in
the air conspiring to determine a life through one powerful gesture. What
does she know?

Only that today, something shifted. Infinitesimal, but an alteration just the
same. Perhaps there really is no crossing long distances, twice. Who she
was when she arrived is not the one who left. And it is just as well.

"Life is short, ask me, I know," he said. It was like a permission, and with a
single fat tear from her devotion, she too, finally believed she could be free.

GRACE

> *"I rest in the grace of the world
> and I am free."*
> —Wendell Berry

The hummingbird flies on to
and from the reed, just enough to remind her
that the reed can bear it.

The baby lands
on the pool and floats
right before panic weighs her down.

The wings of this 737 flaps
at just the right angle
to give it lift.

Tears pause behind
my eyelids just in time
to stop a deluge.

PRAYER

God, if you exist
and have ears, I want nothing
Anymore.

Take what is unjust
And set it free
In the darkness.

Take this black stone
That weighs and weighs
And set it on the mountain

Where it can live
With what can bear it
And endure.

I am weary of expectations
The careless arrivals of
Impersonal visitors

Twins called despair and longing.
God, if you have ears
Listen:

The water breaks on the shore
The woman breaks with it
And she goes on.

When boredom ends
God remembers her.

She is wary of repetition, the scars they
make, friction without purpose.

This: love poised on the edge of a razor blade
blood tastes like honey.

There is no alternate ending. Repetition
is death. She chose life.

CONVERSATIONS WITH MYSELF

What is a month in the age of the universe?
When we move too fast, acquire too much
and avoid what matters
for another day.

What is a day
in an unjust universe?
He lost his job,
her child will starve on a Sunday
when God rests.

You see nothing is simple,
despite what Duterte tells you.
No one should die needlessly for their
country. Everyone should value their
precious lives.

In an unequal universe
lotus eaters sleep too much,
do too little
puts our lives on the line
as they rest in heavy blankets.

We who are condemned to inherit
an earth crawling on its knees,
laid low by blindness and nature's
contingencies, must decide what a
wonderful world it should be...

VI. THE FUTURE IS A COUNTRY I DO NOT LIVE IN

"As one who either knows enough already or knows enough to be perfectly content not knowing."

Mary Oliver

FLOW

Is movement contained in stillness.
In my mind's eye, a river.

Cool diamond surface
glinting in the light.

Below is restive current.
Motion swimming against itself.

For itself. Within: stories. Atoms rippling
in the flow. Passing through...

THE FUTURE IS A COUNTRY I DO NOT LIVE IN

The quiet weeping was induced by the thought of a golden retriever
still below his prime, dying from neglect.

A poet said the quiet is grief's appetite. When death approaches,
when death passes through and sits on your favorite chair. And stays.

She was thinking this when a lizard darted from view.
Green, full-bellied, waiting it seems for her to notice

that nothing in the air and objects around her house are real.
The lampshade with generous light flooding her eyes belong to fiction.

In a house she has not yet built, in a country everyone
is trying to fashion into a better place they can all live in.

She cannot be faulted for shedding tears for a dog that has not yet died,
or a relative scared of passing. It is only because innocence is a precious thing

these objects of affection contain it, and the future is neither innocent nor guilty.
It is merely a stranger indifferent to her speechlessness. To her silence.

To her inability to stop anything with words.

PAUSE

For now, let us close the screens. Let it go dark. The afternoon is beautiful.
The Hollywood hills have never looked

so clear, crystal. For a moment, white clouds hung so low
I mistook them for snow glazing the

mountain peaks. I sometimes wonder what person
I will be once I can hug a friend again. Once

I can sing without a mask. When I can dance without distance.
For now, I bask in the largesse of this

moment. Laptop closed, eyes misty from too much looking.
The light cool air grazes my

nose, uncovered. I am here. Alone before this pause.
Grateful to be alive.

FRACTALS

"We call it a grain of sand,
but it calls itself neither grain nor sand."
Wislawa Szymborska

She sees herself from her mind's eye
woman repeating, repeating.

Sea and foam and sand within
woman praying, weighing, waiting.

She tears her tears into vast water
undulating, receding, residing.

Days and hours that blur as
years. Contained in this moment

inside this old tree, this old sea,
this eternal landscape.

Woman wanting willing shape shifting.
Life breaking open turning and returning.

CLIFFS OF FALL

She read somewhere today that Labradors continue to wag their tails
in suffering, even while dying. They can't help it, a vet said. It's in their nature,
he added. This detail made her weep.

Is it innocence therefore, or helplessness? Something fundamental shifted
in her chest.
Just like the black pebble she has been trying to spit out. She thought.
It has sat on her heart for a considerable time.

Considers her etherized on its table. She thought of all the Labradors in
the world. Said a prayer.
Placed her hand over her mouth. Not to stifle a sob, nor to scatter a scream.
Silence as she reels the answer in.

LEONORA

Carrington swims in a pool with sharks. She long ago decided conventions
are for fools who scoff at mystery. So she swims away.

I consider this as I watch her paint a dead Christ on a canvas.
Eyes gouged out. Mouth half open. Darkness tunneling through his insides.

The king that eats our monsters turned into a monster. I asked her:
why so much deflection? She turns around and winks at me.

Unmasking this stranger. As if to say: you who should know better
ought to jump in that pool and swim today. And I say aye, I say aye.

THE YEAR

I lived entirely in my head, I made up songs of love instead.
I crowed and crooned and hummed and tuned,
yet nothing but my heart did swoon.

The year I lived entirely in my mind, the hours they
marched within a grind. I climbed and climbed and climbed
and climbed, and no walls ever did decline.

Stuck, alive, webbed and wedded to survive.
Captive lizard to my days, ticking, ticking,
in many ways. So I incline.

THE GARDEN

The new arrival considered what it's like to live here:
all love and daylight shutting charcoal clouds out. Perfumed and eager,
her face of white petals considers the lady of the garden:
oblivious but alert, her passion simply to be admired.

Compared to where she came from, this is paradise,
the new arrival mused. Beneath a canopy of crimson,
pink and purple, giant swallowtails and monarch butterflies
part the air, silent wings the breeze rides with a whirl as they tango.
As days and nights wore on, she was happy to part with her origins.
She began to feel at home.

Her heart, emptied of the memory of hands that loved, faces seen.
The air above shifted as she chuckled at a brown anole flexing
its mighty dewlap tongue a blooming orange rose,
blowing an orange kiss in her direction.

MATINS

Remember, waking up at 6am: Your world crystal, a whistle glides on it.
Somewhere, a Bluejays wings hurtled through palm fronds.

& Green anoles sighed at an object of desire.
Rain, needles of it quietly fell on your heart's warm surface.

All the fog in your brain lifted, as a hand from the sky
lifts handfuls of clouds revealing the horizon.

You forgave.
Yourself. And everyone.

HORIZON

It is blue foremost. Cotton blue opens your mouth
to imagine sweet candy clouds filling you.

Then it's white. Bulbs, cotton balls and fists of it.
The bird a fat needle hurtling through the hemisphere.

Clouds so thick your lips fasten, not for sugar but for a scream.
Not ice cream but the cold snare of a sliver of fear. You are here.

DUSK

What does surface smell Iike after it is singed by lightning?
Metal? Elemental? Perhaps it is the aftermath of memory fading from
view, a city you keep leaving but cannot depart from.

Islands unable to contain big emotions on Friday afternoons,
fastening them with words; everything gets entwined.
Suddenly, you decide it is time to leave this day.

It is unlike any other with its pavilions of ghosts, anthologies of childhood
games no longer made for being free.
Let yourself go? P

erhaps a new day awaits to hold you in its embrace. Its arms light as feathers.
Loving your foolish heart.

CATARATA

In moments like these:
hummingbirds calling from your window;
the sun ardent on treetops.

In your mind's eye: an open field. Rawis in the 70s.
Ripe watermelon heads lolling in 90 degree heat.
Rice stalks conspiring with the elements for survival.

On days like this, memory restores.
Not the pain and silence of those who can no longer
speak for themselves, nor the love your heart bore,

not even the courage it took to leave —
But the peace at last of knowing. The smile breaking open
on your face, as though God was just here.

ON A NIGHT

that swallowed stars
her eyes swallowed tears.

Perhaps it is just as well
curtains fall

a story ends & she flips
the switch without regret.

There is a poem in her mind
a woman who looks for

pearls in mud. She knows
too well it is the wrong hand

the wrong eyes the wrong
everything and yet she searches

convinced fidelity to mystery
is her inheritance, twice broken

twice blessed. Captive to
repeat performances

sorrow the size of a stage
on which her morrows are made.

GRISAILLE

*There is an ancient art of layering where a painting is rendered only in
shades of gray.*

In the early days of the pandemic, time was not yet a stranger. Days mere
numbers marked with certainty that there is an end to this.
It is however high noon in January. Long before I knew you too will be
taken. Among the nameless graveyards running out of names.

How does God layer the earth with His dead? This widening canvas
stretched out before His Great Plains. How does He grieve if He grieves
with us? This morning, I felt the knife of sadness as yet again, another life
was taken. First a cough. Then a respirator.

A comma called a coma. Measured silence as machines die on the dead.
Lingering silences inside our never goodbyes. I am trying so hard to
maintain poise and passion in this dark tableau. Walking like a
madwoman so that I can outpace this disease.

Somehow, something keeps catching up. A dark shadow in a trench coat,
headed towards me. Knowledge that loss has altered this landscape.
The alley where I turn is old. All roads travelled by now. Refugees from
grief crowd this highway, slouching towards hope.

Soon, we will head to a city stalked by ghosts. We will again ask for
normal. I will follow your lead and walk the other way...

ABRIENDO

Show me things I cannot see when my eyes are open.
Not darkness but a blank slate punctured by shafts of light.

Show me a world I do not find everyday when the sun dispenses mercy.
Jacaranda blooms rioting on the sidewalk in spring, beauty and madness within.

I want to turn away, but I can't look away. So much commands my
attention these days. Bullets headed in my direction.

They spare neither hours nor days. An endless going on, a zooming in and out
of faces in boxes where my friends wait to live.

Show me a road I can walk on, unbound. Not the road I know,
but the one I missed on a wrong turn long ago. And I will follow.

NOCTURNE

Every single thing on this earth carries a premonition of loss.

That emerald vase you loved so much you stroked it with affection
until the owner sighed in surrender. The platinum ring he slid on your finger until

its circumference began to shrink. The potter's wheel cannot always detect a crack.
Years pass by before clay contrives to show fragility too is its

inheritance. So it is today as you scan the horizon and see nothing
but what used to be there that is always there: The sky, cerulean blue until it's not.

The nightingale so ardent until it flies away. You, turning hands over and over
in a room filled with loss and longing — until it loses you.

FIVE TO FIFTY

"There are places like this everywhere, places you enter as a young girl from which you never return."
—Louise Glück, "Averno"

What she lost when she was five is gone forever. God was asleep when she was taken and did not wake until it was too late. The little girl had disappeared.

This is the arc of their journey together. The Almighty seeking atonement, as she wandered the world, hidden. In fact, she was running away. For a long time, she could not

recognize him in fortune nor misfortune. Deaths. Inaugurations of loss. Wrong weddings. More funerals in between. The demolition of the house where she grew up, cement block by cement block.

Progress skins memory. Replaces it with gloss that cannot stand in for the real thing. As she travelled the world, moon in Rome, dawn in Malaysia, dusk in Burma, God watched from a distance. Give her space, He thought.

In these silent solitary phases, her being cantilevered to its limits. Walking the streets of Bangkok, abandoned child. Barely mothered, barely, clothed. It was a flaying of sorts, those years.

Winter, before she knew it, came early for the girl. It was therefore not a surprise that she ended up in a place where she could choose the seasons. Helicopter years.

Someone swooped in, the hand of omnipotence nudging a peach her way. A man. A boy. A ring. A marriage. Mermaid opening the message in a bottle. Love swept along with it. Boat moored at last. What solid ground felt like.

Girl from the barrio walking under golden California sunshine. Hair grown so long from the absence of seasons, time moving just the same. A ship filled with her ancestors docked safely on a pier, haunts the Pacific.

Ghosts moored in her front yard now. Some days she summons them and they oblige. Other days they love her and calls her name from a hallowed distance. "It's not yet time," they whisper. "You are only just being born

yet again and we are glad to watch your birthing." She turns away from all her longings, feels the stones in her pocket and agrees. Not yet. God let's out a sigh of relief, bearing witness, unaware what she will do next.